Birthdays Around the World

BY JACKIE GLASSMAN

Table of Contents

Where and Why Did Birthday Parties Begin?

No matter who you are or where you live, you have a birthday. Everyone in the world has a birthday. From the games people play to the food they eat, this special day is **celebrated** in different ways by different **cultures**.

How do you celebrate your birthday? If you live in the United States, you probably have a party. Everyone sings "Happy Birthday" as you make a wish and blow out candles on a cake. But where and why did birthday parties first begin?

The first parties were held hundreds of years ago in Europe. Back then, people believed that bad spirits were all around you on your birthday. They thought that if friends and family joined you to celebrate, their good wishes and gifts would scare away the spirits.

Did You Know?

Some people say that birthday candles were first lit to frighten away bad spirits. People made wishes while blowing out the candles because they thought the spirits would be distracted by the change in the light.

How Are Birthdays Celebrated Around the World?

Germany

The day on which each of us was born is a day we celebrate. In some European countries, a tree is planted when a baby is born. It is believed that if the tree grows to be strong and healthy, the child will, too.

In Germany, a baby's birth is recognized with a special birthday candle. It has twelve markings on it. Each year on the child's birthday, the candle is burned down to the next marking.

Say It!

Alles gute zum geburtstag or *Herzlichen gluckwunsch zum geburtstag* means "happy birthday" in Germany.

This birthday cake says ▲ "Happy Birthday" in German.

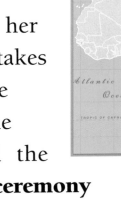

Kenya ▼

Ethiopia ▲

Atlantic Ocean

TROPIC OF CAPRICORN

In Kenya, the mother straps her new baby to her back. She takes the infant to the fields where the cattle are kept. When she gets there, her husband and the village elders have a special **ceremony** to give the child a name.

In the mountains of Ethiopia, just north of Kenya, the news of a baby's birth travels by voice: five shouts for a boy and three for a girl.

◀ Kenyan mothers carry their children on their backs until the children are old enough to walk.

Did You Know?

It is a custom for a mother in West Africa to take her baby for a walk when the baby is eight days old. Friends and family are invited to meet the new baby as mother and child stroll by.

5

Korea
▼

In Korea, families celebrate two important days in a child's life: the 100th day and the first birthday. These days are special because in the past, many babies died before reaching them.

On a first birthday, a Korean baby is said to choose its own future! Objects are put in front of the baby and everyone waits to see which will be picked up. A baby who chooses a book might become a teacher!

Say It!

Sangil chha hamnida means "happy birthday" in Korea.

▲ In Korea, families celebrate with rice cakes and other treats. Games are played and gifts are given.

In Israel, the most important birthday in a child's life is the thirteenth birthday. On that day, the child takes part in a special ceremony. For a boy, it is called the bar mitzvah. For a girl, it is the bat mitzvah. A child prepares for this ceremony for months. On this day, he or she is said to become a grown-up!

Israel

Israeli birthday children sit in a chair decorated with streamers and are lifted high into the air. Party guests dance all around them.

Say It!

Yom Holedet Sameach means "happy birthday" in Israel.

What Are Some Birthday Traditions in Different Countries?

Poland

Birthdays are a time for fun and festivities, and often for other birthday **traditions**. In Poland, everyone's name has a special date on the calendar. This is the person's name day. People celebrate their name day instead of their birthdays.

Name Day in Poland

On this day, the person who is celebrating gives a party. Family and friends bring flowers and gifts. They sing the words "May you live 100 years in health and even longer."

Denmark

Imagine waking up to find presents all around your bed! That is how Danish children begin their birthdays.

Birthdays in Denmark are also celebrated by displaying the Danish flag. If you walk by a house and see the Danish flag hanging in the window, you know someone is having a birthday.

Say It!

Tillykke pa Fodselsdagen means "happy birthday" in Denmark.

Make a Birthday Flag!

You Will Need:
- felt
- scissors
- markers
- glitter
- glue

1. Have an adult help you cut the felt in the shape of a rectangle.

2. Using the markers, glitter, and glue, decorate your flag.

3. On your birthday, hang your flag outside for everyone to see!

In the Netherlands, birthdays that mark even-numbered years of age are called "crown years." In those years, a Dutch child gets an extra-special gift and sits in a chair at the dining table decorated with flowers, balloons, and streamers.

Netherlands

◀ This girl is getting ready to go to her birthday party.

Say It!

Gefeliciteerd means "happy birthday" in the Netherlands.

In Peru, children get a party favor when they go to a birthday party. They also receive a special pin made to honor the day. Many children collect these popular pins. Each guest gets a fancy paper hat as well. The birthday child's hat is in the shape of a crown, of course.

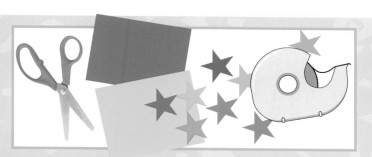

Say It!

Feliz cumpleaños means "happy birthday" in Peru.

Make a Peruvian Crown!

Peruvian children enjoying candy.

You Will Need:
- scissors
- 2 sheets of construction paper
- tape
- star-shaped foil stickers

1. Cut a crown shape along the top of both sheets of construction paper.

2. Tape the two strips together to form the crown. Make sure it fits around your head.

3. Decorate the crown with the stars.

What Foods Do People Eat on Their Birthdays?

Ghana

Atlantic Ocean

Birthdays might mean birthday cake to you, but not to children in Ghana. There, birthday boys and girls wake up to a special breakfast dish of mashed sweet potatoes and eggs fried in palm oil. Later at the party, guests feast on a sweet treat made of fried plantains, which are like bananas. Yum!

Make a Sweet Treat!

You will need:
- 3 pounds plantains (cooking bananas)
- 2 teaspoons ground red pepper
- 1/2 tablespoon salt
- 1 teaspoon powdered ginger
- 2 tablespoons water
- 3 cups oil

1. Wash and peel the plantains.
2. Mix red pepper, salt, and ginger with water. Drop the plantain slices into the mixture and stir.
3. Have an adult place the plantains into oil and deep-fry them until golden brown.

Say It!

Medzi dzigbe njkeke nyuie no wo is "happy birthday" in Ewe Tribal language in Ghana.

In Morocco, people gather with members of their family to celebrate a birthday. There is usually a feast of their favorite foods followed by a birthday cake.

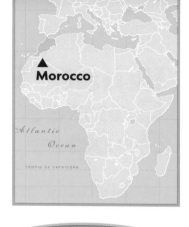

Morocco

Atlantic Ocean

TROPIC OF CAPRICORN

Say It!

Eeid milad sa'eed means "happy birthday" in Arabic.

◀ These Moroccan children are celebrating a birthday.

What Birthday Games Do People Play?

Mexico

At birthday parties, children have fun playing games. In Mexico, children play a game called **piñata**. The piñata is a decorated container, often shaped like an animal. It is filled with candy and toys and hung from a tree or other high place. Children are blindfolded and spun around. They try to break open the piñata with a stick. When they are successful, everyone runs to get the treats.

To make the game harder, the piñata is raised and lowered with a rope.

Nigeria

A favorite birthday party game in Nigeria is "Pass the Parcel." It's a game like "Hot Potato," except that you want to be left holding the parcel at the end. When the music stops, the child holding the parcel unwraps a layer. When the music begins again, the parcel is passed on once more. Whoever gets to unwrap the final layer wins the prize inside.

Say It!

Eku ojobi means "happy birthday" in Nigeria.

▲ This is a Nigerian girl on her birthday.

Did You Know?

In Nigeria, some birthday years are very special ones. These include years 1, 5, 10, and 15. On these birthdays, kids often have huge parties with up to 100 guests.

Birthdays All Around

Asia

In Asia, there are many ancient traditions surrounding birthdays. Many Asian cultures use a lunar calendar that has twelve different animal signs. The animal for the year in which a child is born is said to have great influence on the child's life.

Say It!

Tanjoubi omedetou means "happy birthday" in Japan.

◀ To celebrate their birthdays, these girls are dressed in kimonos (kih-MOH-nohz).

Did You Know?

In Japan, the most important birthdays are the third or the seventh for a girl, and the fifth for a boy. On those birthdays, the children have a ceremony called the "Seven, five, three." They dress up in their best clothes and get special candies that say "Sweets for 1,000 years of life."

Animal Signs of the Asian Lunar Calendar

Years Born	Animal	What It Means
1912, 1924, 1936, 1948, 1960, 1972, 1984, 1996		The rat is imaginative, charming, and generous.
1913, 1925, 1937, 1949, 1961, 1973, 1985, 1997		The ox is very confident and a born leader.
1914, 1926, 1938, 1950, 1962, 1974, 1986, 1998		The tiger is sensitive, emotional, and loving.
1915, 1927, 1939, 1951, 1963, 1975, 1987, 1999		The rabbit is imaginative, smart, and generous.
1916, 1928, 1940, 1952, 1964, 1976, 1988, 2000		The dragon is popular and likes everything to be perfect.
1917, 1929, 1941, 1953, 1965, 1977, 1989, 2001		The wise and charming snake is romantic and a deep thinker.
1918, 1930, 1942, 1954, 1966, 1978, 1990, 2002		The horse is hardworking, intelligent, and friendly.
1919, 1931, 1943, 1955, 1967, 1979, 1991, 2003		The goat is elegant, artistic, and fun to be around.
1920, 1932, 1944, 1956, 1968, 1980, 1992, 2004		Everyone likes the monkey because of its intelligence and good humor.
1921, 1933, 1945, 1957, 1969, 1981, 1993, 2005		The rooster is a hard worker and a good decision maker.
1910, 1922, 1934, 1946, 1958, 1970, 1982, 1994, 2006		Honest and faithful, the dog never lets down those it loves.
1911, 1923, 1935, 1947, 1959, 1971, 1983, 1995, 2007		The boar is sincere, honest, and smart.

In Ecuador, people don't celebrate their birthdays on the day they were born. Instead, they have a party on the day of the **saint** for whom they are named. In other parts of the world, such as Italy and Mexico, children often celebrate on both their birthday and their saint's day. That means they get two parties!

These Ecuadorian girls are celebrating a friend's quinceañera, her fifteenth birthday. This is a special day for girls in many Latin American countries, and their families give large parties for them.

In the United States, people celebrate the birthdays of great leaders in the nation's history. George Washington, Abraham Lincoln, and Martin Luther King Jr. each have a day of their own. When is your birthday? How do *you* celebrate?

United States

Did You Know?

People who are born on February 29 don't have a birthday every year. The last day in February is usually the 28th. February 29 occurs only in leap years. A leap year is a year that can be divided by four.

In England, Australia, and New Zealand, everyone gets a day off to celebrate the birthday of the queen. Although Elizabeth II was born in April, her birthday is celebrated in June!

Martin Luther King Jr.

Abraham Lincoln

George

Queen Elizabeth II

GLOSSARY

celebrated (SELL-uh-bray-did): did something enjoyable on a special occasion, such as having a party

ceremony (SAIR-uh-moh-nee): a public occasion that celebrates a special event or anniversary

cultures (KULL-cherz): beliefs and traits of racial, religious, or social groups

piñata (pihn-YAH-tah): a decorated container filled with candies and toys

saint (SAYNT): a man or woman honored by the Christian church because of his or her holy life

traditions (truh-DIH-shun): information, beliefs, or customs of a generation or culture

INDEX